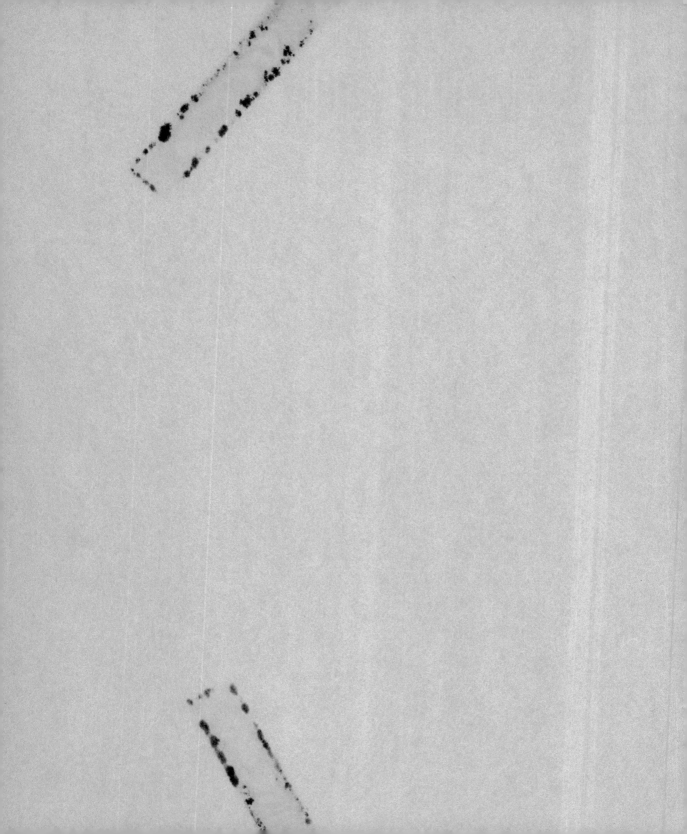

JEWISH HOLIDAYS

by Margery Cuyler

JEWISH HOLIDAYS

illustrated by Lisa C. Wesson

Holt, Rinehart and Winston   New York

24758

10 9 8 7 6 5 4 3 2 1

Library of Congress Cataloging in Publication Data

Cuyler, Margery.
  Jewish holidays.

  SUMMARY: Describes the rituals connected with the Jewish holidays throughout the year and gives instructions for making a variety of related objects from easily available materials.
  1. Fasts and feasts—Judaism—Juvenile literature. [1. Fasts and feasts—Judaism. 2. Handicraft]
I. Wesson, Lisa. II. Title.
BM690.c89   296.4′3   77-10801   ISBN 0-03-039936-x

"An Only Kid" from *The New Haggadah for the Pesach Seder,* edited by Mordecai M. Kaplan, Eugene Kohn, and Ira Eisenstein. Copyright 1941 by Behrman House, Inc., New York. Used with permission of Behrman House, Inc.

"Kol Nidre" prayer from *The High Holiday Prayer Book,* translated and arranged by Ben Zion Bokser. Copyright © 1959 by Hebrew Publishing Company, New York. Used with permission of Hebrew Publishing Company.

"Neilah" prayer from *The High Holiday Prayer Book,* translated and arranged by Ben Zion Bokser. Copyright © 1959 by Hebrew Publishing Company, New York. Used with permisssion of Hebrew Publishing Company.

Prayer for earth-grown fruit and prayer for wine from *The Prayer Book (Weekday, Sabbath, And Festivals),* translated and arranged by Ben Zion Bokser. Copyright © 1957, 1961 by Hebrew Publishing Company, New York. Used with permission of Hebrew Publishing Company.

"Rock of Ages" from *Hanukkah, The Feast of Light,* compiled and edited by Emily Solis-Cohen Jr. Copyright 1937, 1965 by the Jewish Publication Society of America. Used with permission of The Jewish Publication Society of America.

*The author would like to
thank all the people who helped her
with this book, especially
Miriam Chaikin and Leah Robinson.
M.C.*

*to Berns and all my family
L.C.W.*

Contents

Introduction

All Jewish holidays, except Rosh Ha-shanah and Yom Kippur, celebrate nature or a historic event in the Jewish past.

Most Jewish holidays are based on the holy days mentioned in the Torah, the Jewish book of law (also the first five books of Moses in the Bible). But unlike holidays that celebrate just one person, such as George Washington, Jewish holidays honor the Jewish people as a whole. For example, in ancient days, Jews were forced to pray to the gods of the Syrians, who ruled their country. One Jewish family, the Maccabees, felt this was unfair. They felt so strongly that they risked their lives by organizing a small army to defeat the Syrians. The story of Hanukkah, the holiday celebrating this event, shows how the Jews fought bravely, as a group, for the freedom to worship as they wanted.

In general, Orthodox, Conservative, and Reform Jews do many of the same things on each holiday. They have passed down their rich holiday customs and folklore from generation to generation.

8

Hebrew Calendar

Months	Hebrew Month	Holidays
September	Tishri	Rosh Ha-shanah Yom Kippur · Sukkot
October	Heshvan	
November	Kislev	Hanukkah
December	Tevet	
January	Shevat	Tu Bi-shevat
February	Adar	Purim
March	Nisan	Passover (Pesach)
April	Iyyar	Yom ha-Azma'ut Lag Ba-omer
May	Sivan	Shavuot
June	Tammuz	
July	Av	Tishah be-Av
August	Elul	

Rosh Ha-shanah

Rosh Ha-shanah is the Jewish New Year. It comes on the first day of the first Hebrew month, *Tishri,* which falls usually in September.

Unlike most New Year's days, which are times of joy and celebration, Rosh Ha-shanah is a serious occasion. It is known as a *High Holy Day*, and begins a period of ten "holy days" of solemn worship. On Rosh Ha-shanah, Jews believe each person is judged in Heaven for past good and evil deeds. Everyone's acts and thoughts for the previous year have been written in the *Book of Life.* On Rosh Ha-shanah, the Book of Life is said to be opened and read so that each person's fate for the New Year can be decided. If someone has acted wrongly, it is likely that he or she will be punished during the coming year. But if that person asks to be forgiven, it is possible for the judgment to be changed in the next ten days. This is why on Rosh Ha-shanah and the ten days that follow, Jews ask to be forgiven for their sins. They want to be written down for a good year. Jewish New Year's cards are often called *Shanah Tovahs.* They usually say

Leshanah Tovah Tikatevu, which is Hebrew for "May you be written down for a good year."

On Rosh Ha-shanah eve, the family gathers for a meal before going to the synagogue. After a blessing, they eat

11

hallah, a white braided loaf of bread, dipped in honey. Some families dip apples in honey. This is because everyone hopes for a sweet life in the New Year. Another favorite dish is *tzimmes,* a stew made from meat, prunes, carrots, and sweet potatoes.

Services are held in the synagogue for the next two days. The *shofar,* or ram's horn, is blown at the beginning of the morning service. It gives out a strange, hollow sound. In the olden days, the shofar was blown at all important events—such as when an army was about to attack or a new king was being crowned.

Since Rosh Ha-shanah is a holiday of forgiveness, *Selihot,* or prayers of forgiveness, are said during the service. There is also an afternoon service called *Tashlikh,* based on an old Jewish folk custom. Where possible, people gather near a flowing body of water and throw in breadcrumbs. The crumbs stand for the sins they want to "wash away."

The next holiday, *Yom Kippur,* comes ten days later. Like Rosh Ha-shanah, it is a High Holy Day.

Shanah Tovah Card

What you need:

1. Card paper. Construction paper, typewriter paper, or thin cardboard will do.
2. Felt-tip markers, colored pencils, paints, or crayons.
3. Glue.

What you do:

1. Fold the paper in half.
2. Draw, paint, or paste a picture from a magazine on the front. The picture should have something to do with Rosh Ha-shanah. It might be a picture of hallah, or a shofar.

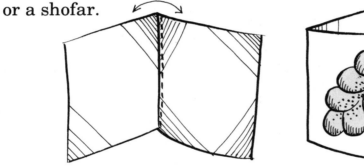

3. Write HAPPY NEW YEAR across the front.
4. On the inside, write *Leshanah Tovah Tikatevu* and sign your name.

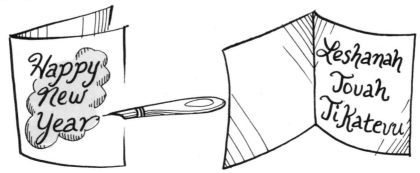

Yom Kippur

Yom Kippur is the holiest day of the Jewish year. It is the day on which the judgment made about each person on Rosh Ha-shanah is sealed, or made final, in the Book of Life.

On this holiday, everyone except small children and sick people fasts. They stop eating and drinking until sunset on the following day. Jews spend this time thinking about the meaning of Yom Kippur.

On the eve of Yom Kippur, there is a service at the synagogue. The *Torah* is placed in the open for people to see. Then the *Kol Nidre* service begins. The Kol Nidre is a famous prayer of forgiveness that is beautifully chanted. Many years ago, the Spanish Jews were forced to become Christians. They had to go to church, even though they didn't want to. At home, they secretly prayed as Jews and begged God to forgive them for acting like Christians. In the Kol Nidre prayer, Jews ask God to forgive them for breaking promises they couldn't keep because of events beyond their control. This is the prayer:

Kol Nidre

All vows, renunciations, promises, obligations, oaths, taken rashly, from this Day of Atonement till the next, may we attain it in peace, we regret them in advance. May we be absolved of them, may we be released from them, may they be null and void and of no effect. May they not be binding upon us. Such vows shall not be considered vows; such renunciations, no renunciations; and such oaths, no oaths.

Services begin early on Yom Kippur day and last until evening. Several times, everyone says out loud a prayer called *Al Het*. In this prayer, they ask once again to be forgiven for every possible kind of sin. They also say a prayer, *Yizkor*, in memory of relatives and friends who have died.

Then in the afternoon, the story of Jonah is read. God told Jonah to go to the city of Nineveh. God wanted Jonah to tell the citizens their city would be destroyed because of their sins. But instead, Jonah sailed off on a ship. God was so angry, He sent a storm to destroy the ship. Jonah was tossed overboard and swallowed by a huge fish. He prayed to God to forgive him, and the fish spit him up onto dry land. Then Jonah went to Nineveh, as God had asked him to do in the first place. He told the people of Nineveh their city was going to be destroyed. The people were terrified and asked God to forgive them. God finally decided to save the city. This story shows God will forgive people for their sins if they ask

Him to. That is why the story of Jonah is read on Yom Kippur—it is a story about forgiveness.

The last service of the day is called *Ne'ilah*. The people chant:

Open, Lord, Thy mercy's door,
The mighty day is done,
Lead us, Lord, into Thy grace,
We see the setting sun.
Gracious God, Thy mercy grant,
Erase the stain within,
Remove the burden of our guilt,
Release our life from sin.

Then the shofar is blown—a signal that the holiday is over.

Jonah Storybook

What you need:

1. Paper. Construction paper, typewriter paper, or blank notebook paper will do.
2. Felt-tip markers, colored pencils, or paints.
3. Stapler.

What you do:

1. Draw a scene from the story of Jonah on each piece of paper, so that together the pictures will make a book.
2. Make a drawing for the cover. Write BOOK OF JONAH across the top.
3. Put the drawings in the right order, with the cover picture first.
4. Staple everything together on the left side. Now you have your own storybook about Jonah!

Sukkot

Sukkot comes a few days after Yom Kippur and lasts for eight days. The word "sukkah" means booth or tent. In ancient days, when the Jews escaped from slavery in Egypt, they made rough huts out of branches. They used these huts for shelter when they camped for the night in the wilderness. Later, when they settled in Canaan, Jewish farmers built tiny huts out of tree branches. They dwelled in them while they brought in their crops.

This holiday reminds Jews of their ancestors' difficult escape from Egypt. It is also a thanksgiving for all things that grow. On Sukkot, Jews build a branch house outside the synagogue. The walls are built with sweet-smelling branches. The roof is made of twigs, through which the stars can be seen. Then ripe fruits and vegetables are hung from the sides and roof. Jews sometimes build branch houses in their backyards and eat their meals in them.

People gather together in the synagogue to thank God for all things that grow. Then they walk around it carrying four kinds of plants. The branches of palm, myrtle,

19

and willow trees are tied together and held in the right hand. The citrus fruit, or *etrog,* is held in the left hand. There are many explanations for why these plants are chosen. Some legends describe the fruit as meaning the following: The palm, or *lulav,* produces good fruit, but it doesn't smell. This stands for the Jew who knows the Torah but doesn't go out of his or her way to be kind and honest. The myrtle, or *hadas,* smells good but has no taste. It stands for people who are kind to others but have not read the Torah. The willow, or *aravah,* does not smell or have any taste. It stands for Jews who are unkind and do not follow the teachings of the Torah. Etrog looks like a large lemon. It smells good and has a delicious flavor. It stands for people who have read the Torah and are kind and warm toward others.

When these plants are not being used during a service, they are placed outside the branch house.

The eighth day of Sukkot is called *Shemini Azeret.* Special services for people who have died are held in the synagogue, and more prayers are said for rain. These prayers have an important meaning in Israel, where rain is needed in the fall to yield a good harvest in the spring.

Then the *Simhat Torah* is held, usually on the ninth day. The rabbi and several people at the service take the Torah scrolls and march with them around the synagogue. The reading of the Torah goes on all year. But on this day, the last chapter is finished, and the first chapter started all over again. Children are allowed to read out loud next to the grown-ups. They also carry special flags and parade seven times around the synagogue. Before they go home, children are given candy, cake, and fruit. The next holiday isn't for another two months.

Sukkot Table Decoration

What you need:

1. Lidless shoebox.
2. Scissors.
3. Paints, crayons, or felt-tip markers.
4. Sticks and leaves.

What you do:

1. Draw a door on one side and cut it out.
2. Draw, paint, or paste magazine pictures of ripe fruit, leaves, and branches on the sides.
3. Place leaves and twigs loosely across the open top.

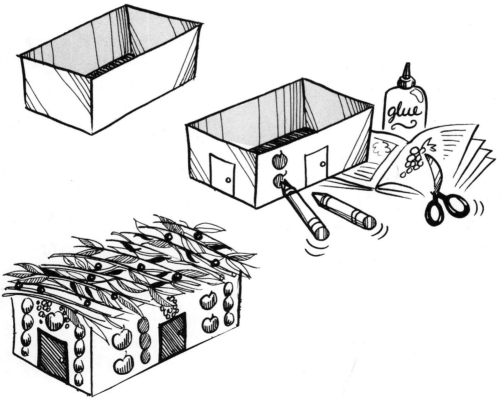

Hanukkah

Hanukkah is known as the "Festival of the Lights."

More than two thousand years ago, the land of Israel was ruled by the Syrians. The Syrians believed in the Greek religion. Their evil king, Antiochus, tried to force the Jews to give up their beliefs and worship Greek gods. He sent his soldiers into the Temple at Jerusalem. There, they slaughtered pigs as a gift to one of their gods, Zeus. They placed a statue of him on the altar. The Temple, the holy shrine in which Jews worshipped their one god, was no longer pure.

But Antiochus was still not satisfied. He sent his soldiers back to the Temple. They stole or destroyed beautiful things and put up statues of more Greek gods. They left the Temple in shambles. Many Jews were tortured, and Jewish women and children were sold into slavery. One brave Jewish family, the Maccabees, decided to fight back. They fled to the mountains and formed an army to battle the Syrians. The Syrians attacked them many times, sometimes on elephants. The Jews used bows and arrows. Even though the Maccabees were

fewer in number, they were smart and ambushed the enemy over and over. Finally, they defeated the Syrians. Then they left the mountains to return to the Temple in Jerusalem.

They were heartbroken when they saw the statues of Greek gods and goddesses everywhere. Dirt and blood covered the floor. The Jews rebuilt the altar and cleaned the Temple. According to legend, when they tried to relight the *menorah,* or candleholder, they could find only a tiny bit of pure oil—enough to last for just one day. By some miracle, the oil burned for eight days. And that's why Hanukkah is celebrated for eight days. Each night, a candle is lit in the home to remind Jews of the oil that kept the candles burning in the Temple so long ago.

The first candle in the menorah is lit at sundown when the holiday begins. Each night, another candle is lit. By the eighth night, all eight candles are burning. An extra candle, or *shammash,* is used to light the other candles, and it stays lit each night. The candles are placed near a window so they can be seen from the street.

This holiday is a favorite of Jewish children. On the first night, they receive a small amount of money called *Hanukkah gelt.* They also play a game with a *dreidel.* The dreidel is a spinning top that has four Hebrew letters on it. They are the first letters of the four words *Nes Gadol Hayah Sham,* which means "A great miracle happened there." This refers to the miracle of the pure oil burning in the Temple for eight days during the time of the Maccabees. The Jews also used the dreidel in ancient days to trick the enemy into thinking they were playing harmless games. Actually, they were busily studying the Torah; they only put it away and brought out their dreidels when they heard the enemy coming.

A lot of good food is eaten during the eight days of Hanukkah. Potato *latkes,* or pancakes, are a great favorite. They remind the Jews of the Maccabee women who cooked latkes for the Jewish soldiers when they were battling the Syrians so long ago. Also, songs are sung, such as "Rock of Ages." The words are:

> *Rock of ages, let our song praise Thy saving power;*
> *Thou amidst the raging foes, wast our sheltering*
> *tower.*
> *Furious they assailed us, but Thine arm availed us,*
> *And Thy word broke their sword when our own*
> *strength failed us.*

Dreidel Games

Gimmel Takes All

1. Each player puts a nut in the center of the table or floor.
2. Next, each player spins the top.
3. When it stops, the players look at what letter is turned up.
4. If *Nun* is up, the player gets nothing.
   If *Gimmel* is up, the player wins all the nuts.
   If *Hay* is up, the player gets half the nuts.
   If *Shin* is up, the player adds a nut to the center.
5. Each spin is a game. Play as many games as you want.

Highest Number Wins
1. The four letters stand for numbers.
   Gimmel = 3
   Hay = 5
   Nun = 50
   Shin = 300
2. The players agree before the game starts on a number that they want to reach.
3. Then they spin the dreidel, and the first person to reach the number wins.

Spin the Dreidel
The player whose dreidel spins for the longest period of time wins.

Tu Bi-shevat

This holiday is known as the "New Year of the Trees." When *Tu Bi-shevat* is celebrated, it is springtime in Israel, and trees are being planted. Since the soil there is very dry, trees do not grow as easily as in America. That's why on Tu Bi-shevat Jews pray that the new trees being planted in Israel will be healthy.

Jews also believe trees stand for what is good and strong. Sometimes the Torah is called the "Tree of Life."

In ancient days, a cypress tree was planted when a daughter was born. If the baby was a boy, the father planted a cedar tree. When the children grew up and married, their tree branches were cut and used to hold up the cloth the bride and groom walked under at their wedding.

Today, schoolchildren buy leaf stickers and paste them onto a tree drawing. When the tree is filled with stickers, the money used to buy them is sent to Israel to purchase a tree. Then a tree is planted for the good of Israel in the name of the children.

Lots of delicious foods are eaten on Tu Bi-shevat,

especially fruit that can be grown in Israel. *Bokser* (carob tree fruit) is a favorite. Also, oranges, dates, figs, pomegranates, almonds, lemons, and grapefruit.

Tu Bi-shevat Tree

What you need:
1. Paper towel tube.
2. Shoebox and lid.
3. Colored paper.
4. Scissors.
5. Pencil.
6. Paints, crayons, or felt-tip markers.
7. Scotch tape.

What you do:
1. Trace the round bottom of the paper towel tube on the middle of the lid.
2. Make a hole by cutting out the circle you've traced.
3. Put the lid on the box.
4. Color the tube.

(turn the page to finish your tree)

5. Stick the tube through the hole.

6. Roll a piece of colored paper into the shape of a tube and fasten the edges with Scotch tape.

7. Cut strips, five inches long, into one end of the paper tube.

8. Put the paper tube inside the cardboard tube, leaving the end with strips sticking out.

9. Fold the strips over the edge of the cardboard tube so they look like tree branches.

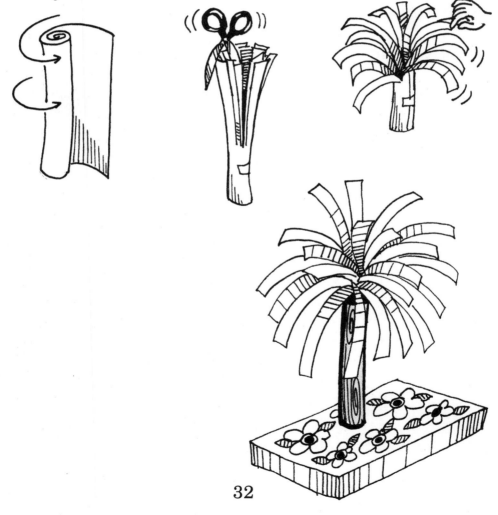

Purim

This holiday celebrates an event in the life of a clever queen named Esther. The story is written in a scroll called the *Megillah*. On *Purim* eve, people flock to the synagogue to hear the Megillah read.

According to the story, the king of Persia became angry at his first wife and decided to remarry. He held a beauty contest and picked the loveliest girl, Esther, to be his bride. He did not know she was Jewish. Her cousin and guardian, Mordecai, advised her not to tell anyone about her family or people. Even though most Persians had nothing against the Jews, there were some who didn't like them. Mordecai was afraid that if those people found out Esther was a Jew, they might persuade the king not to marry her.

After the marriage took place, Mordecai overheard two soldiers by the palace gates plotting to poison the king. He told one of the king's officers about it, and the two soldiers were caught before they could carry out the murder. Mordecai's name was written down in the royal book of records for having saved the king's life.

While Esther was queen, the king decided to appoint a new prime minister. He picked a man named Haman, who expected everyone to bow before him. Some people did, but Esther's cousin, Mordecai, refused to do so.

Haman was furious. He decided Mordecai was a trouble-maker and should be killed, and that all Persian Jews should be killed along with him. In order to pick a lucky day to carry out his wicked plan, Haman cast lots. It is believed he did this by throwing small stones or sticks onto the ground, the way dice are used today. When the lot landed on what he considered to be a lucky place, he made his decision: The day on which he'd carry out his evil deed would be the thirteenth day of the Jewish month of Adar. "Purim" is the ancient word for lots.

When Mordecai heard about Haman's plan, he rushed to tell Queen Esther. Only she could stop Haman and save the Jews!

They met in secret, and he told her a clever idea: If she let the king know she was Jewish, then surely he would stop Haman from killing the Jews. Esther thought it over. She was worried the king might be angry at her for not having told him she was Jewish in the first place. But she also knew she had the power to save her people. She told Mordecai she needed strength. She felt if the Jews fasted for three days and prayed for her success, God would hear their prayers. Then she'd feel brave enough to tell her husband she was Jewish.

Mordecai agreed that three days of fasting and pray-ing would help. So he, Esther, and all the Persian Jews fasted and prayed for three days. At the end of that time, Esther felt brave enough to see the king. When he heard what she had to say, he was not angry. In fact, he was thankful Haman's evil nature had been revealed. He also remembered how Mordecai had once saved his life. And so he had Haman and his ten sons hung from the gallows! Then he made Mordecai the new prime minister, and everyone was happy.

Purim begins on the fourteenth day of Adar. Some people start fasting at sunrise the day before. This is called the Fast of Esther. But at the synagogue service on Purim eve, the holiday becomes more joyous. This is because Purim is considered a happy occasion. Everyone wants to celebrate Esther's victory. Children dress in costumes and act out her story. They hold *gragers,* or noisemakers, and twirl them when they hear Haman's name. They also boo, hiss, and stamp their feet. They do everything they can to drown out Haman's evil name.

People also give each other gifts and money. They especially remember the poor. This is because after Mordecai became prime minister, he insisted the first Purim holiday be for both rich and poor.

Toward evening, Jews gather for a splendid Purim feast. The most popular treat is called *hamantaschen.* These are little cakes, with three corners, filled with prunes or poppy seeds and honey. Some say the shape is like the hat that Haman wore, and also looks like one of his pockets. Others say it resembles the shape of his ear.

Make Your Own Grager

What you need:
1. Two paper cups.
2. Felt-tip markers or pictures from magazines or newspapers.
3. Pebbles.
4. Stapler.
5. Paste or glue.

What you do:
1. Draw some designs or paste pictures on the outside of the cups.
2. Fill one cup with pebbles.
3. Turn the other cup over on top of the first one, so the open ends are face to face.

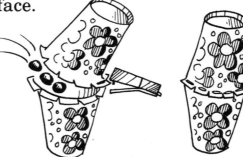

4. Staple the edges of the open ends together. You may have to bend the edges out a little to get the staples in.
5. Now shake your grager.

Passover (Pesach)

When the Jews lived as slaves in Egypt thousands of years ago, they were forced to serve the Egyptian king, or Pharaoh. Pharaoh ordered them to plow the fields and become servants in Egyptian homes. He made them build enormous buildings in the hot sun. They had to work from dawn to dusk without rest. God sent two messengers—Moses and his brother Aaron—to beg Pharaoh to free the Jews. But Pharaoh didn't want to lose his slaves and refused to free them. For this, he and the Egyptian people were punished with ten plagues:

1. The river was turned to blood.
2. Frogs leapt out of the river and covered the land.
3. Egyptians and their animals were covered with lice that made them itch.
4. Wild beasts entered the land.
5. Livestock became sick and died.
6. Boils broke out on the Egyptians' skin.
7. A terrible hailstorm ruined crops.
8. There was a plague of flies and locusts.

9. It became dark for three days.
10. The firstborn child and calf of every Egyptian family was killed.

The tenth and last plague was by far the worst. God had told Moses that every Jewish family should prepare a lamb and bring it as an offering to Him, and Jewish parents should smear the lamb's blood on their doorposts. This was so the Almighty would pass over their homes and not kill any Jewish children or animals. The term *Passover* comes from this event.

After the tenth plague, Pharaoh gave in and agreed to let Moses and Aaron lead the slaves out of Egypt.

It was a very hard journey. The Jews did not even have time to pack bread. Instead, they packed unrisen bread dough, which they baked into flat cakes under the hot desert sun.

While they were camping out in crude huts in the wilderness, Pharaoh decided he had made a mistake. In letting the Jews go, he had lost thousands of slaves. So he ordered his army to recapture the Jews.

The only hope for the Jews lay in crossing the Red Sea, or Sea of Reeds, to safety. They prayed for help from God. Then, a miracle happened. God divided the Red Sea water so the Jews could walk across dry land to the other side. But when the Egyptian soldiers followed them, the water came together, and the soldiers drowned.

Passover, based on this story, is a holiday that cele-

brates freedom. It reminds the Jews of the time in history when their ancestors were freed from slavery.

It is also a harvest festival, since most Jews became farmers when they finally reached Canaan. On the second day of Passover, they began the harvest of cereals by bringing an omer (ancient measure) of barley, the first cereal to ripen, to the Temple. The farmers said a special prayer over each omer for fifty days, until the wheat, or last cereal to ripen, was cut.

Passover is honored as a pilgrim festival too, since years ago Jews journeyed to Jerusalem to celebrate Passover. There they would sacrifice a lamb as a Passover offering.

Jews observe this holiday for eight days. On the first two nights of Passover, the family gathers together for a special and important meal called a *Seder*. Seder means "order," and a very strict order is followed during the meal. The table is set with the family's best tablecloth, china, wine glasses, and silver. Many Jews have a separate set of everything just for the Passover days.

Jews eat certain types of food when the Seder starts. Each kind is related to the flight of the Jews from Egypt. This special food is carefully arranged on a richly decorated Seder plate. There is a hard-boiled or roasted egg, a roasted lamb bone, greens, bitter herbs, and *haroset*. There are also three pieces of *matzah,* each wrapped in a special napkin. In addition, parsley, greens, and cups of salt water are placed on the table for everyone to share. Here are some of the reasons these particular foods are eaten:

1. HARD-BOILED EGG: The hardness of the egg stands for the strength of the Jews.

2. ROASTED LAMB BONE: This is a reminder of the lambs that were killed so that God would "pass over" the Jewish homes during the tenth plague. It also stands for the lamb that was sacrificed in ancient days before the destruction of the Temple.

3. SALT WATER: This stands for the tears shed by the Jewish slaves in Egypt. It is also like the salty Red Sea.

4. GREENS: Parsley and celery are dipped into the salt water as a reminder of the parting of the Red Sea. These greens also stand for springtime.

5. BITTER HERBS: Sometimes called *maror,* these herbs are horseradish roots. Eating maror recalls the suffering of the Jewish slaves.

6. HAROSET: Made from wine, chopped apples, cinnamon, and nuts, it is a reminder of the clay mixture the slaves used for making bricks for Pharaoh.

7. MATZAH: This is a flat bread made without any salt or yeast. It is like the bread the Jews baked when they were in the wilderness. The three pieces on the plate stand for the three different Jewish groups that were slaves in Egypt: Kohanim, Levites, and Israelites. The fact that they all stayed together and didn't forget their Jewish religion while in Egypt was one reason they escaped successfully.

No bread other than matzah can be eaten in a Jewish home during Passover. The home is swept and cleaned to remove all traces of leavened bread (bread that has risen). When the holiday begins, breadcrumbs are placed on a windowsill in a special ceremony. With a feather, they are swept into a wooden spoon, and a blessing is said. They are then burned the next morning.

During the Seder, the family leader sits on a soft pillow at the head of the table. Everyone reclines, or sits in a relaxed position, as free men did in ancient times. Then the Seder leader says a blessing, or *kiddush,* over the wine, recognizing the holiness of the day. Everyone drinks, after saying this blessing: "Praised be Thou, O Lord our God, King of the universe, who createst the fruit of the vine." (Children often drink grape juice instead of wine.) Next, the Seder leader pours water over his hands without saying the usual hand-washing blessing. Then he dips the greens into the salt water and passes them around for all the people at the table to taste. Before they eat, they say: "Praised be Thou, O Lord our God, King of the universe, who createst the fruit of the earth."

After this, the leader breaks the middle piece of matzah in two and hides one half. This is the popular *afikoman*, which is searched for playfully by the children later on. (When a lamb was no longer sacrificed at the Temple in ancient times, a piece of matzah was eaten instead. This was called the afikoman, the Greek word for dessert.)

Now it is time for the youngest child at the Seder to ask four questions:

1. Why does everyone eat matzah?
2. Why does everyone eat bitter herbs?
3. Why is food being dipped in salt water?
4. Why is everyone reclining?

In answer to these questions, the head of the family reads aloud from a book called the *Haggadah*—which in Hebrew means legend or story. Each person has a copy. Besides telling what the Passover food stands for, it tells the story of how Moses led the Jewish slaves out of Egypt. It reminds people of how God saved their ancestors from being destroyed. Everyone is free to interrupt and ask questions while the Haggadah is being read.

Then everyone washes his or her hands and says the usual blessing before the meal. The blessings before eating bread and matzah are also said. Next, each person eats two pieces of matzah, broken off from one of the pieces that's still covered. Another blessing is said over the bitter herbs and then they are tasted. They are also dipped into the haroset for sweetness, and eaten as a sandwich on a piece of matzah.

Now it is time to eat the rest of the meal. Families decide for themselves what to eat during this part of the Seder. *Gefilte fish* is a favorite. It is a mixture of boiled freshwater fish chopped up, shaped into balls, and served cold.

As the meal draws to a close, the children begin to look for the afikoman. Usually, the head of the family gives a small gift to the child who finds it. The afikoman is then divided among the guests. No more food is eaten after this, so that the taste of matzah stays in everyone's mouth.

When the meal is finished, the door is opened so the invisible prophet, Elijah, can enter. Even though he can't be seen, everyone likes to think he joins the Seder and drinks a glass of wine that has been especially set aside for him on the table. He is one of the Jews' favorite prophets and stands for hope.

The Seder ends with prayers of thanksgiving and songs. One favorite song is called *Had Gadya,* or "An Only Kid." This is a folk song about a father who bought a kid—a little goat—for a small amount of money (two zuzim*). Even though the song starts with the goat getting eaten by a cat, it ends with the "Holy One." Some say the ending means God will do away with evil so the world will become a better place in which to live. Here are the words:

An Only Kid

An only kid!   *Then came the cat*
An only kid!   *And ate the kid*
My father bought   *My father bought*
For two zuzim.*   *For two* zuzim.
An only kid! An only kid!   *An only kid! An only kid!*

* *Ancient coins.*

Then came the dog
And bit the cat
That ate the kid
My father bought
For two zuzim.
An only kid! An only kid!

Then came the stick
And beat the dog
That bit the cat
That ate the kid
My father bought
For two zuzim.
An only kid! An only kid!

Then came the fire
And burned the stick
That beat the dog
That bit the cat
That ate the kid
My father bought
For two zuzim.
An only kid! An only kid!

Then came the water
And quenched the fire
That burned the stick
That beat the dog
That bit the cat
That ate the kid
My father bought
For two zuzim.
An only kid! An only kid!

Then came the ox
And drank the water
That quenched the fire
That burned the stick
That beat the dog
That bit the cat
That ate the kid
My father bought
For two zuzim.
An only kid! An only kid!

Then came the shohet*
And slaughtered the ox
That drank the water
That quenched the fire
That burned the stick
That beat the dog
That bit the cat
That ate the kid
My father bought
For two zuzim.
An only kid! An only kid!

Then came death's angel
And slew the shohet
That slaughtered the ox
That drank the water
That quenched the fire
That burned the stick
That beat the dog
That bit the cat
That ate the kid
My father bought
For two zuzim.
An only kid! An only kid!

Then came the Holy One,
   praised be He,
And destroyed death's angel
That slew the shohet
That slaughtered the ox
That drank the water
That quenched the fire
That burned the stick
That beat the dog
That bit the cat
That ate the kid
My father bought
For two zuzim.
An only kid! An only kid!

* The ritual slaughterer.

Shavuot

The word "shavuot" means weeks. The holiday *Shavuot* comes in late spring, seven weeks after Passover. It honors three things.

First, it celebrates the fruit harvest in Israel and is sometimes known as the "Holiday of the First Fruits" (*Hag Ha-Bikkurim*). In ancient days, farmers brought their first ripe fruits to the Temple as an offering of thanks. American Jews celebrate the ripening of the first fruits in Israel by decorating their homes with flowers and leaves.

Second, it is a holiday for the wheat harvest. Long ago, the cereal harvest began on the second day of Passover, when each farmer brought an omer (ancient measure) of barley to the Temple. Shavuot was celebrated fifty days later, when the wheat had ripened and was ready to be cut. It is sometimes called the "Festival of the Harvest" (*Hag Ha-Katzir*).

Third, it falls at the time Moses climbed Mount Sinai and heard the Ten Commandments from God. They are written in the Torah and form the basis of the Jewish

religion. Shavuot has a third name—"The Time of the Giving of Our Law" (*Zeman Mattan Torahtenu*).

On this holiday, the Scroll of Ruth is read in the synagogue. Ruth was a brave woman who lived in Moab, a country near the land of Israel. One year, when there was little rain and the crops in Israel had failed, two Jewish brothers moved to Moab. There, one of them met and married Ruth. During her marriage, Ruth accepted the Jewish religion as her own. When her husband died, she followed her mother-in-law back to Bethlehem. She arrived during the harvest and gathered in grain to make a living for both of them. Ruth's story is a good choice for Shavuot because much of it took place during the harvest season.

Many Jews include a new ceremony in the synagogue on Shavuot. It is a graduation ceremony, or *confirmation*. It is for the boys and girls who have completed their studies in religious schools. In this ceremony, they become full members of the Jewish faith.

After the Shavuot services, there is a holiday dinner. Ripe fruit and other good foods are served. Cheese blintzes and cheesecake are eaten because they are dairy foods, and the Law of God is known as "honey and milk."

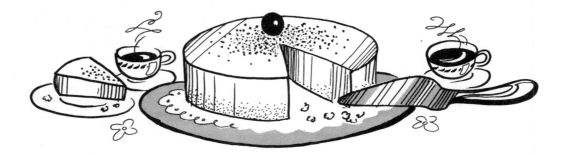

Shavuot Fruit Decoration

What you need:

1. A piece of styrofoam.
2. Toothpicks.
3. Aluminum foil.
4. Ripe fruit.

What you do:

1. Wrap the aluminum foil around the styrofoam.
2. Cut the fruit into small pieces.
3. Stick the fruit into the styrofoam with toothpicks. It is fun to make a pretty design with the fruit.

Note: You can also add parsley, watercress, or lettuce around the bottom.

Shabbat

Most holidays happen only once a year, but *Shabbat* happens once a week. That is why many people do not think of it as a special holiday. Still, it is very important because one of the Ten Commandments says: "Remember the Sabbath day to keep it holy." It is also the oldest of all the Jewish holidays and is often referred to as a bride or queen, because it is welcomed with happiness. The Jews believe God worked very hard for six days to create the world and rested on the seventh day. This is why Shabbat falls on Saturday, which is the last day of the week on the Hebrew calendar. (The word "shabbat" means rested in Hebrew.) Shabbat starts on Friday evening.

Not all Jews treat this holiday in the same way, however. Some people go to the synagogue for services both Friday night and Saturday. Some do not turn on any lights in their house on the Sabbath. This is because in ancient times lighting lights was hard work. The custom of not turning on lights in modern times is a way of stating that no one should work on the Sabbath.

But almost all families have a special meal at home on Friday night after sunset. The table is set with a clean white tablecloth and the best family dishes. Two loaves of bread (*hallot*) and a cup of wine are placed next to a pair of candles. The mother lights the candles and says a special prayer:

Blessed art Thou, O Lord our God, King
of the universe, who hast sanctified us by
Thy commandments, and has instructed us
to kindle the Sabbath lights.

The father then says kiddush, the blessing over the wine. Then he blesses the bread and says a special blessing for the children.

The family often eats gefilte fish. Soup, roast chicken, and *kugel,* or pudding, are also eaten.

Shabbat is one of the only times the family can get together each week and pray. It is a time set aside for everyone to relax and rest. This is one reason most people go out of their way to celebrate it with a special meal.

Hallah Cover

What you need:

1. A piece of white material big enough to cover a basket of hallot. A large handkerchief will do.
2. Crayons or felt-tip markers.

What you do:

Draw candles, wine decanters, or a pretty Shabbat design on the cloth. Or, you may just wish to write the word "shabbat" in Hebrew: שבת

Other holidays

Yom ha-Azma'ut: This is Israel Independence Day. It is the newest of all the Jewish holidays and falls on the fifth day of Iyyar. It is in honor of the day on which the modern state of Israel was founded on May 14, 1948.

Lag Ba-omer: This holiday is sometimes called the "Scholars' Holiday" in honor of the deeds of two rabbis, Rabbi Akiva and Rabbi Shimon bar Yohai.

Almost two thousand years ago, when the Romans wanted to take over the Temple in Jerusalem, Rabbi Akiva's students joined the Jewish leader Bar Kokhba in fighting against them. Unfortunately, many of the student-soldiers were killed by a plague. However, on the thirty-third day of the omer counting between Passover and Shavout, the plague mysteriously disappeared. Bar Kokhba's army was able to fight for a few more years, before being defeated by the Romans. In Hebrew, Lag Ba-omer means "Thiry-three days of the counting of the omer."

During this same time, Rabbi Shimon bar Yohai

taught the Jews the Torah, even though the Romans told him not to. He was finally caught, and he and his son had to hide in a cave. Twelve years later, he was able to leave the cave and return home to continue teaching the Torah.

Tishah be-Av: This holiday recalls the tragic things that have happened to Jews in the past. Jews are especially sad over the two times their Temple was destroyed: once by the Babylonians in 586 BCE, and once by the Romans in 70 CE. Both times, it is believed the Temple was destroyed on the ninth day of the Jewish month Av.

On this day, the *ark*, or cabinet holding the Torah in the synagogue, is sometimes draped in black. Everyone recites sad hymns and prayers, and passages are read from the Book of Jeremiah. Jeremiah lived during the destruction of the First Temple. In his writings, he mourns the sorrow of the Jews at that time.

Some Jews look at this holiday differently. They think of all the people who died during the War of Independence in 1948. They treat Tishah be-Av more as a day of hope, a day that celebrates the fact Israel is a nation.

Glossary

Adar The sixth month of the Hebrew calendar.

Afikoman A piece of matzah the head of the family hides during the Seder meal on Passover.

Al Het A prayer of forgiveness people say out loud on Yom Kippur.

Aravah The willow branch that is tied to palm and myrtle branches and carried in the right hand on Sukkot.

Ark The cabinet in the synagogue that holds the Torah.

Av The eleventh month of the Hebrew calendar.

Bokser Carob tree fruit eaten on Tu Bi-shevat.

Book of Life The book in Heaven in which the thoughts and deeds of each person are recorded during the year. On Rosh Ha-shanah, each person is judged for the coming year, based on what has been written in the Book of Life for the previous year.

Confirmation A graduation ceremony, celebrated on Shavuot, in which boys and girls who have completed their studies in religious schools become full members of the Jewish faith.

Dreidel A spinning top used on Hanukkah which has four Hebrew letters on it. They are the first letters of the four words "Nes Gadol Hayah Sham," which means "A great miracle happened there." This refers to the miracle of the pure oil in the Temple during the time of the Maccabees.

Elul The twelfth month of the Hebrew calendar.

Etrog The citrus fruit carried in the left hand during Sukkot.

Gefilte fish A mixture of boiled freshwater fish formed into balls and often eaten on Passover and Shabbat.

Gimmel One of the four Hebrew letters on a dreidel.

Grager A noisemaker that a child shakes on Purim to drown out Haman's name.

Hadas The myrtle branch that is tied to willow and palm branches and carried in the right hand on Sukkot.

Had Gadya A favorite song sung at the end of the Seder.

Haggadah A book on the Seder table that tells the story of how, in ancient times, Moses led Jewish slaves out of Egypt to freedom. It also tells what the Seder food stands for.

Hag Ha-Bikkurim The "Holiday of the First Fruits," celebrated as part of Shavuot.

Hag Ha-Katzir The "Festival of the Harvest," celebrated as part of Shavuot.

Hallah A loaf of braided bread glazed with egg white.

Hallot The plural of hallah.

Hamantaschen Little cakes with three corners, filled with prunes or poppy seeds and honey, eaten on Purim.

Hanukkah The "Festival of Lights." Each night for eight days, candles are lit in the synagogue and home, one candle to mark each day. This is in honor of the Maccabees, a Jewish family who led an army against the Syrians in ancient days. They found only enough pure oil in the Temple to burn for one night. The oil lasted for eight days, which was considered a miracle.

Hanukkah gelt A small amount of money given to children on the first night of Hanukkah.

Haroset A special food eaten at the Seder. It is made out of wine, chopped apples, cinnamon, and nuts.

Hay One of the four Hebrew letters on a dreidel.

Heshvan The second month of the Hebrew calendar.

High Holy Days Rosh Ha-shanah and Yom Kippur.

Iyyar The eighth month of the Hebrew calendar.

Kiddush The blessing said over the wine on Shabbat or Passover.

Kislev The third month of the Hebrew calendar.

Kol Nidre A prayer of forgiveness chanted on Yom Kippur.

Kugel Pudding, often eaten on Shabbat.

Lag Ba-omer A holiday that honors the deeds of two rabbis—Rabbi Akiva, whose students fought bravely under Bar Kokhba against the Romans, and Rabbi Shimon bar Yohai, who taught Jews the Torah during the time they were ruled by the Romans.

Latkes Special pancakes. Potato latkes are eaten on Hanukkah.

Lulav The palm branch that is tied to willow and myrtle branches and carried in the right hand on Sukkot.

Maror Bitter herbs eaten on Passover.

Matzah Flat bread made without salt or yeast and eaten on Passover.

Megillah The scroll that tells the story of Queen Esther, read in the synagogue on Purim.

Menorah A special holder for the nine candles that are lit during Hanukkah. One of them, the shammash, is used to light the other eight.

Ne'ilah The last service on Yom Kippur.

Nisan The seventh month of the Hebrew calendar.

Nun One of the four Hebrew letters on a dreidel.

Passover (Pesach) Based on the story of how Moses led the Jewish slaves out of Egypt, this holiday celebrates freedom. It is also a harvest holiday and honors the pilgrimages made to the Temple on Passover in ancient times.

Purim A holiday based on the story written in the Scroll of Esther. An evil Persian prime minister named Haman tried to murder the Persian Jews thousands of years ago. The clever Jewish queen, Esther, and her cousin, Mordecai, learned of his plan and found a way to save the Jews.

Rosh Ha-shanah The Jewish New Year. On this High Holy Day, each person is judged in Heaven for past good and evil deeds. On this and the following ten days, people ask to be forgiven for all their sins.

Seder A very important and special meal eaten on the first and second nights of Passover.

Seder plate A special plate on the Seder table which contains bitter herbs, a hard-boiled or roasted egg, greens, haroset, three pieces of matzah, and a roasted lamb bone.

Selihot Prayers of forgiveness on Rosh Ha-shanah.

Shabbat A weekly holiday that starts on Friday evening and ends on Saturday. It celebrates the seventh day on which God rested after creating the world.

Shammash A special candle used to light the eight other Hanukkah candles.

Shanah Tovah card The short name for a Happy New Year card, sent on Rosh Ha-shanah.

Shavuot A holiday that celebrates three things: (1) the fruit festival in Israel (Hag Ha-Bikkurim); (2) the wheat harvest (Hag Ha-Katzir); and (3) the Ten Commandments (Zeman Mattan Torahtenu).

Shemini Azeret The eighth day of Sukkot. Special services are held in the synagogue for people who have died. Prayers are also said for rain, in hopes that there will be a good harvest in Israel.

Shevat The fifth month of the Hebrew calendar.

Shin One of the four Hebrew letters on a dreidel.

Shofar A trumpet made of a ram's horn and blown in the synagogue on Rosh Ha-shanah and Yom Kippur.

Simhat Torah Usually held on the ninth day of Sukkot, a service in which the rabbi and several people march around the synagogue with the Torah scrolls. The Torah is read out loud by both grown-ups and children.

Sivan The ninth month of the Hebrew calendar.

Sukkot A harvest holiday in which a branch house is built outside the synagogue or home.

Tammuz The tenth month of the Hebrew calendar.

Tashlikh Part of the afternoon service on Rosh Ha-shanah, based on an old folk custom. Where possible, people gather and throw breadcrumbs into a body of flowing water. These crumbs stand for sins they want to wash away.

Tevet The fourth month of the Hebrew calendar.

Tishah be-Av A holiday in memory of the two times the Temple was destroyed in ancient times, once by the Romans and once by the Babylonians. It is also a day that honors Israel as a nation.

Tishri The first month of the Hebrew calendar.

Torah The Jewish book of law; it is the first five books of Moses in the Bible.

Tu Bi-shevat The "New Year of the Trees," celebrating the planting of trees in Israel.

Tzimmes A stew made from meat, prunes, carrots, and sweet potatoes and often eaten on Rosh Ha-shanah.

Yizkor A Yom Kippur prayer honoring the memory of relatives and friends who have died.

Yom ha-Azma'ut Israel Independence Day, which honors the founding of the modern state of Israel on May 14, 1948.

Yom Kippur The holiest Jewish holiday, in which people ask to be forgiven in Heaven for their sins.

Zeman Mattan Torahtenu "The Time of the Giving of Our Law," in honor of when Moses heard the Ten Commandments. It is celebrated as part of Shavuot.

Index